write and play major scales

By **Mary Elizabeth Clark**
and **David Carr Glover**

David Carr Glover
PIANO LIBRARY

Foreword

The main purpose of the format of this book is to stimulate the <u>student's mental picture of scales on the keyboard</u>. The student is to write the finger numbers on a keyboard as well as to write the scales on the staff. Writing the sharps and flats in front of the notes reinforces the picture of black and white keys.

After the student has done the written work, the book becomes a reference and may be used indefinitely for that purpose. Even though students are expected to know scales without a book, it gives them a security to have a reference when needed.

Contents

F.D.L. 324

Scale Forms

There are many scales used in music. In this book you will study and play the kinds of scales used the most in piano music.

Chromatic

The chromatic scale is all half-steps. There are twelve half-steps in one octave.

Whole Tone Scale

The whole tone scale is all whole steps with six whole steps in one octave. There are two whole tone scales.

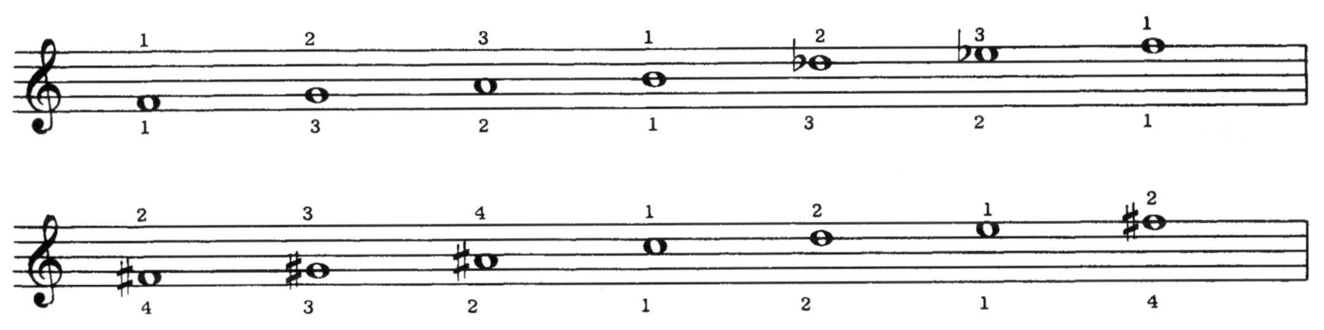

Major And Minor Scales

Major and minor scales are made up of patterns of both whole steps and half steps. These patterns are presented in the book as you study each kind of scale.

Major and minor scales are DIATONIC scales. Diatonic means that every letter name is used in consecutive order; no letter name is repeated; no letter name is omitted. You will note that the chromatic and whole tone scales are not diatonic.

F.D.L.324

Half Steps and Whole Steps

The keyboard is made of half-steps and whole steps. A half-step is from one key to the next key with no key in between. A whole step is from one key to another key with one key in between.

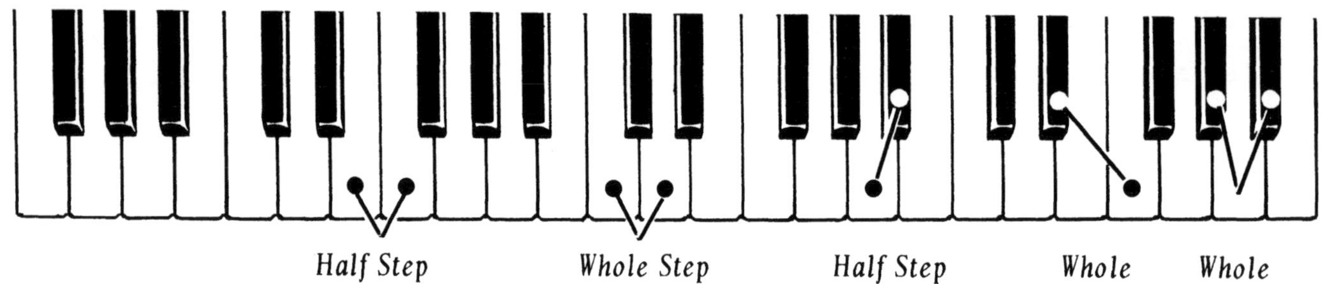

Write H for half-step and W for whole step under the following pairs of notes. Work at the keyboard.

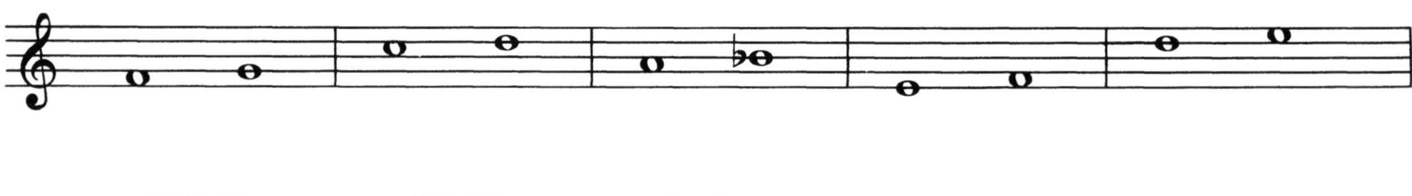

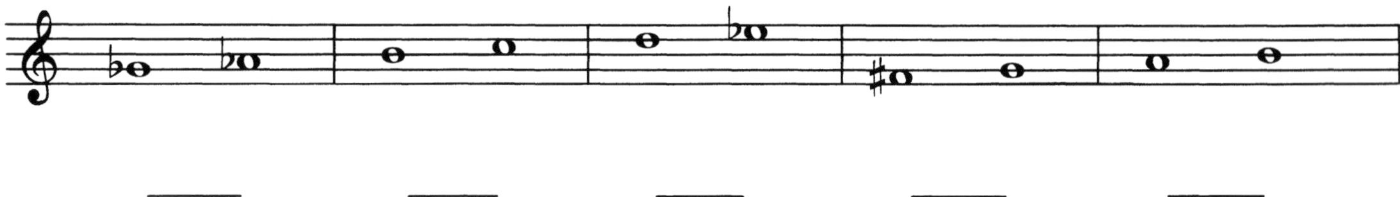

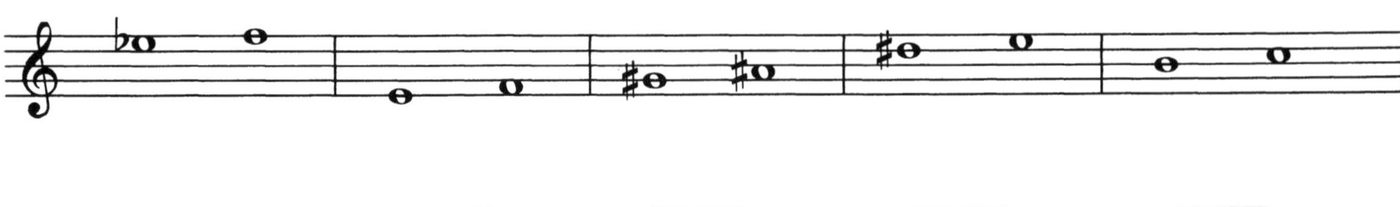

Major Scales

A Major Scale is a series of tones arranged alphabetically in a pattern of whole steps and half steps. The half steps are between 3 and 4, 7 and 8. All other steps are whole steps. The tones of a scale are called degrees.

Pattern of the Major Scale:

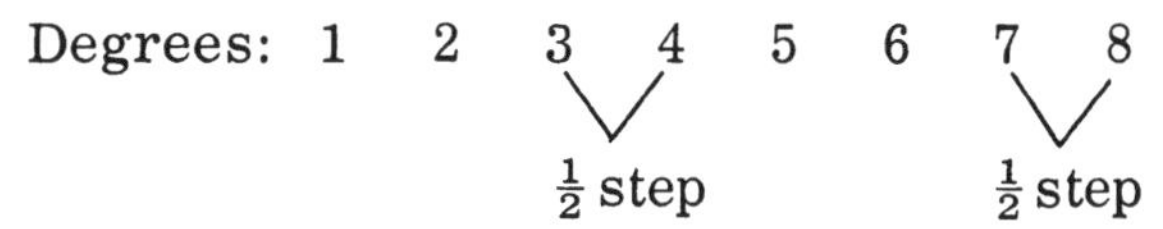

C Major Scale on the Keyboard

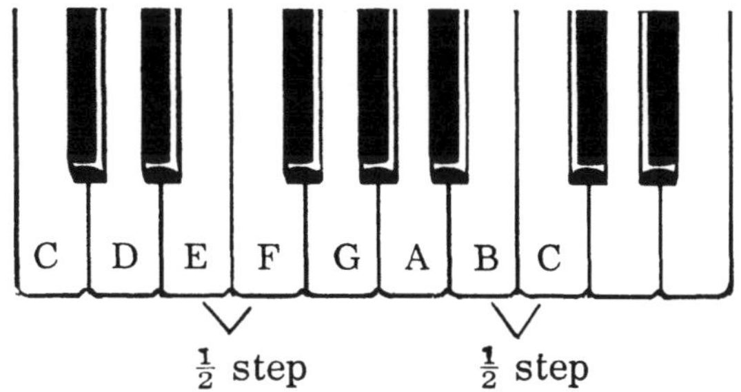

C Major Scale on the Staff

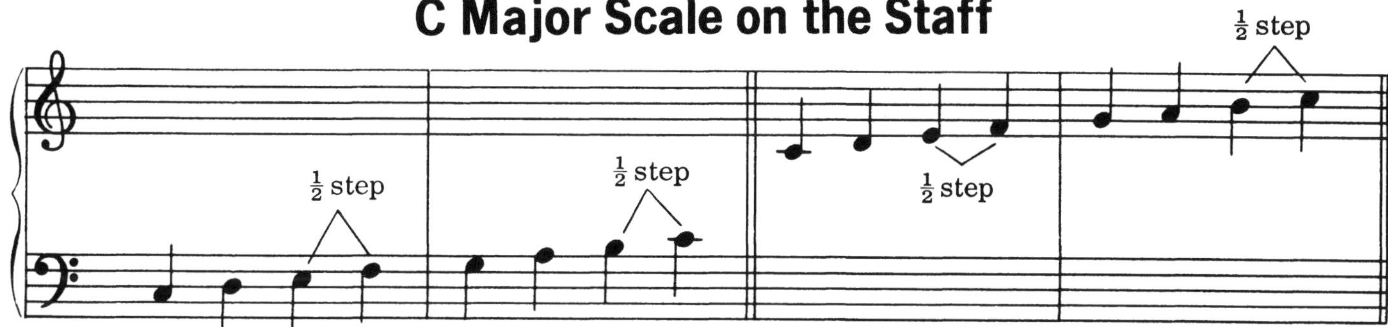

G Major Scale on the Keyboard

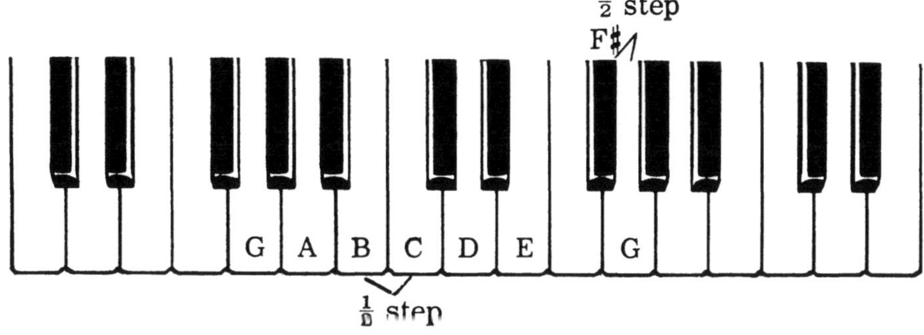

G Major Scale on the Staff

C Major Scale

This is the C Major Scale on the staff for the Right Hand. It is written out for you as an example. You are to write the other Major Scales.

This is the C Major Scale fingering on the keyboard for the Right Hand. This scale is written out for you as an example.

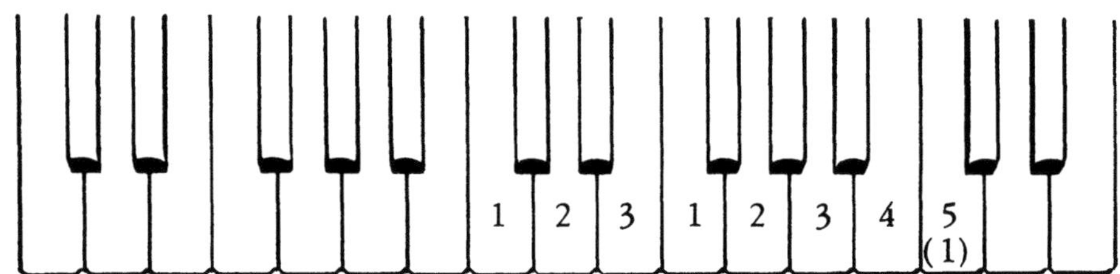

Write the C Major Scale on the staff for the Left Hand, ascending and descending.

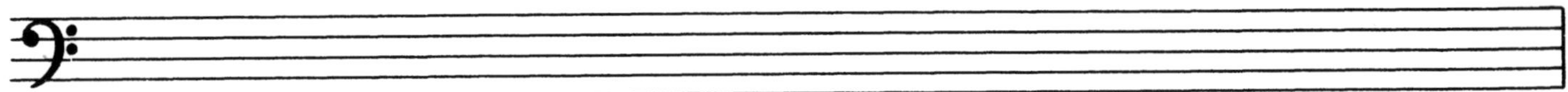

Write the fingering for the C Major Scale on the keyboard for the Left Hand. Refer to Pages 22 and 27 for fingering.

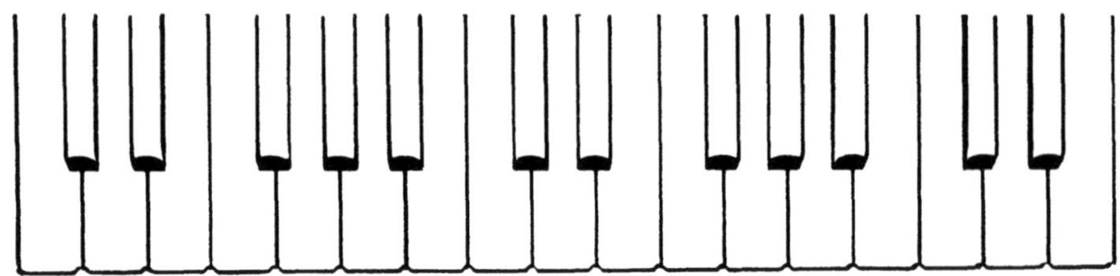

The Key Signature for C Major is no sharps or flats.

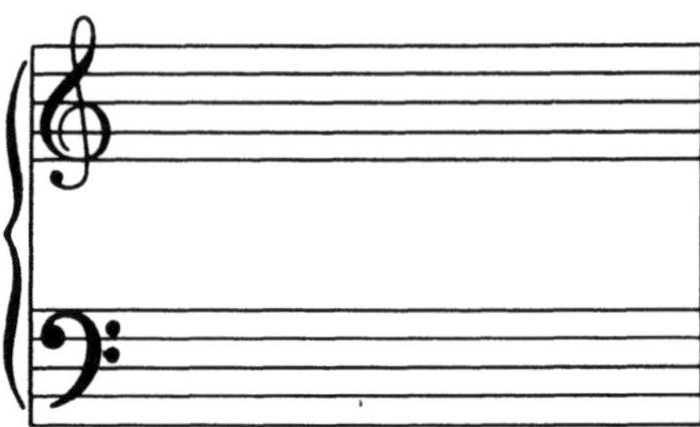

G Major Scale

As you write the sharp major scales you will note that each scale starts on the fifth tone of the preceding scale and uses a new sharp on the seventh tone in order to have the half-step between 7 and 8.

Write the G Major Scale on the staff for the Right Hand, ascending and descending. Write the necessary sharp in front of the note.

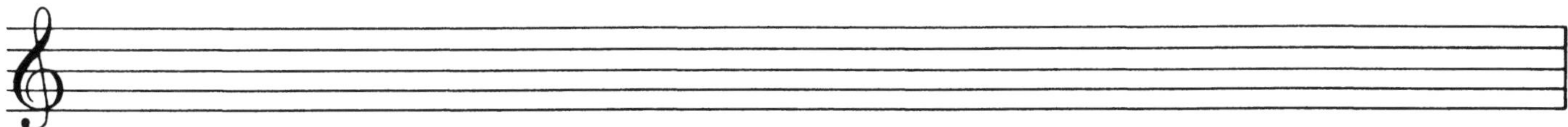

Write the fingering on the keyboard for the G Major Scale for the Right Hand.

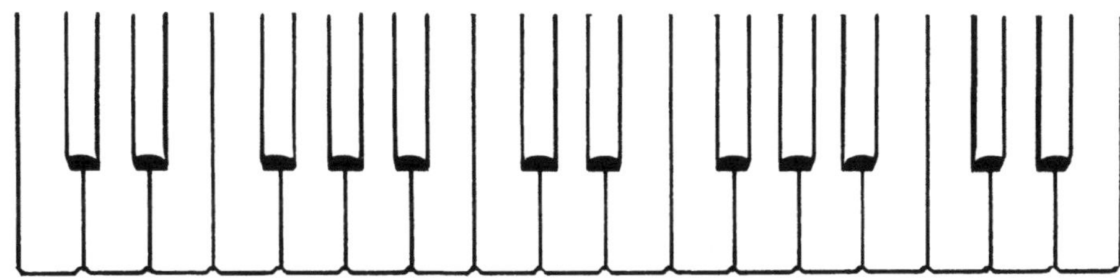

Write the G Major Scale on the staff for the Left Hand, ascending and descending.

Write the fingering on the keyboard for the G Major Scale for the Left Hand.

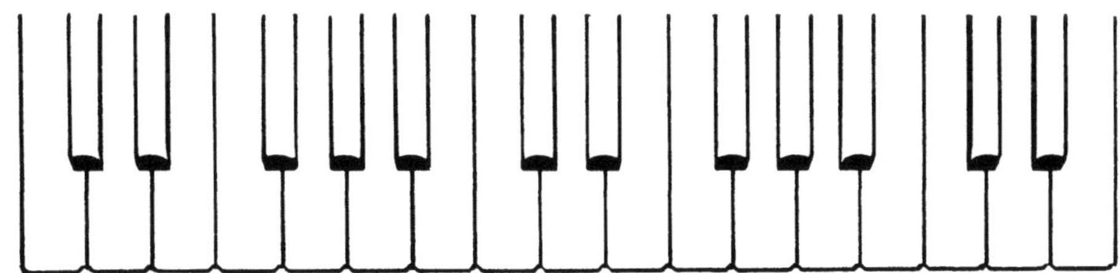

Write the Key Signature for G Major.

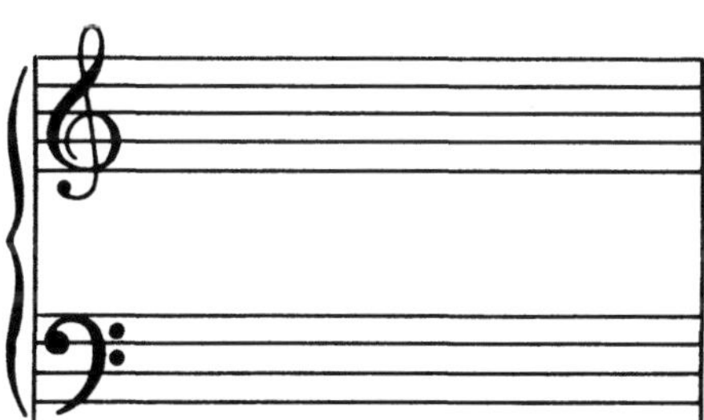

D Major Scale

Write the D Major Scale on the staff for the Right Hand, ascending and descending. Write the necessary sharps in front of the notes.

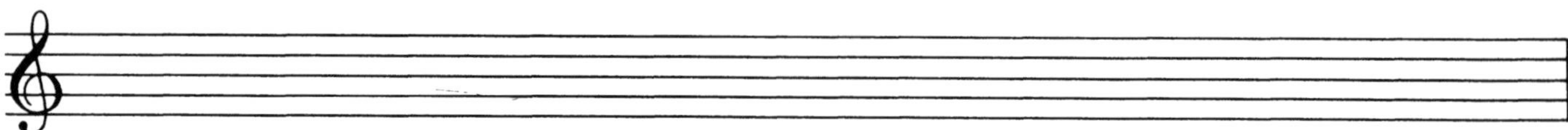

Write the fingering on the keyboard for the D Major Scale for the Right Hand.

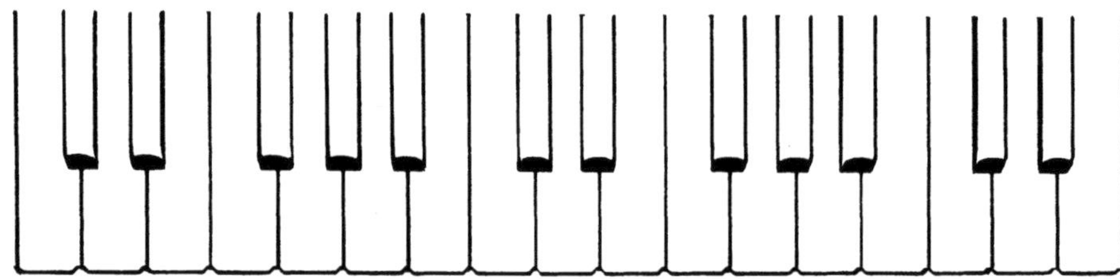

Write the D Major Scale on the staff for the Left Hand, ascending and descending.

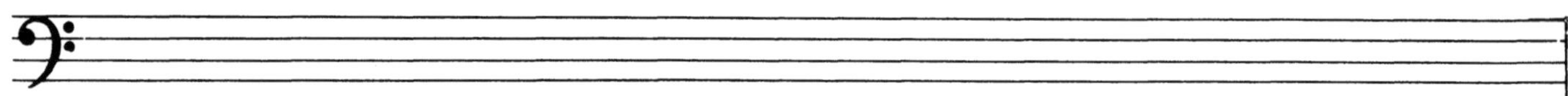

Write the fingering on the keyboard for the D Major Scale for the Left Hand.

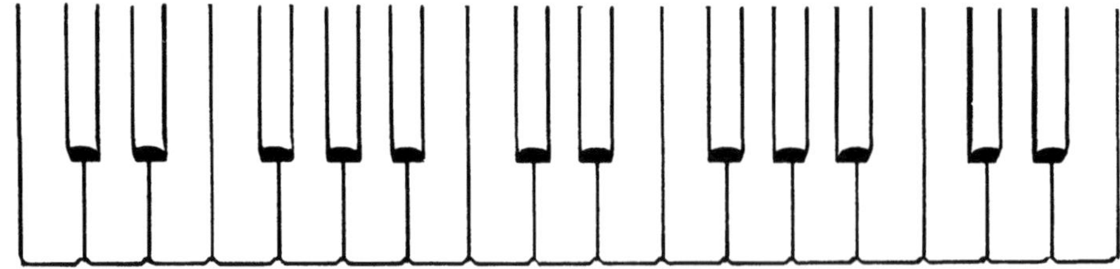

Write the Key Signature for D Major.

F.D.L.324

A Major Scale

Write the A Major Scale on the staff for the Right Hand, ascending and descending. Write the necessary sharps in front of the notes.

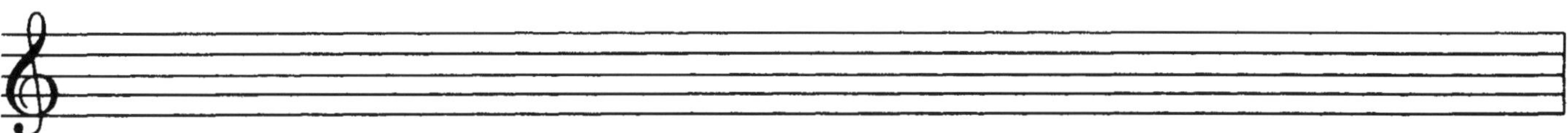

Write the fingering on the keyboard for the A Major Scale for the Right Hand.

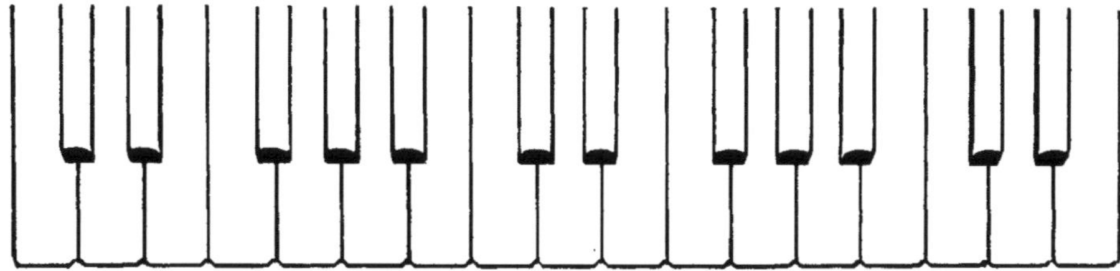

Write the A Major Scale on the staff for the Left Hand, ascending and descending.

Write the fingering on the keyboard for the A Major Scale for the Left Hand.

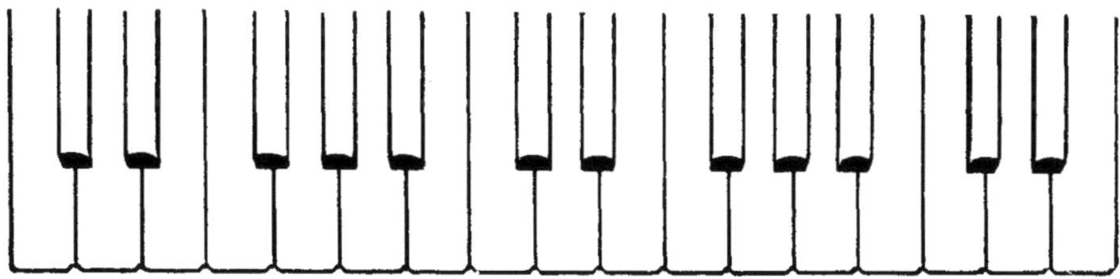

Write the Key Signature for A Major.

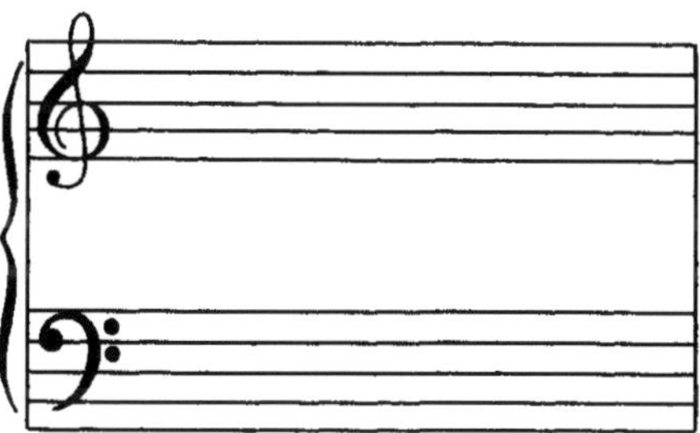

E Major Scale

Write the E Major Scale on the staff for the Right Hand, ascending and descending. Write the necessary sharps in front of the notes.

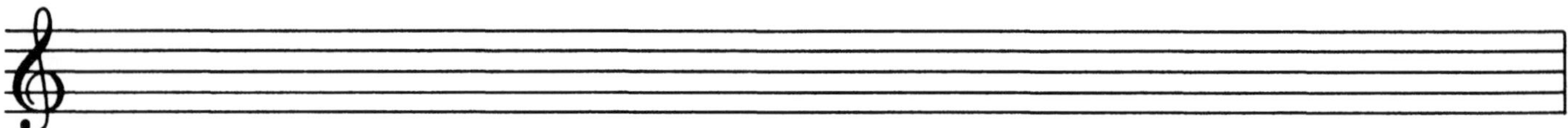

Write the fingering on the keyboard for the E Major Scale for the Right Hand.

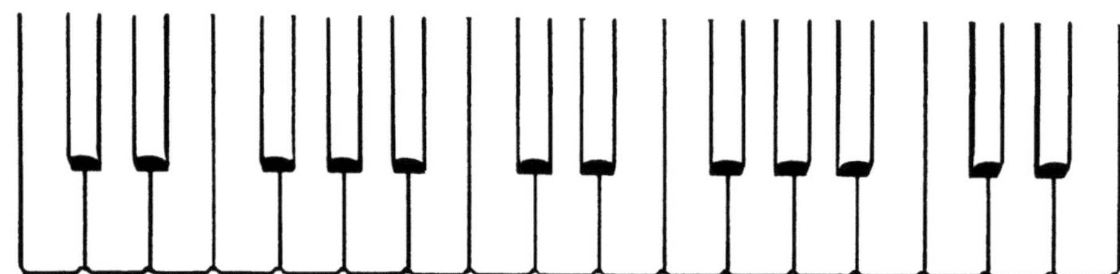

Write the E Major Scale on the staff for the Left Hand, ascending and descending.

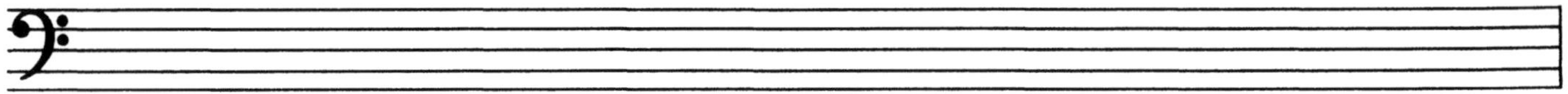

Write the fingering on the keyboard for the E Major Scale for the Left Hand.

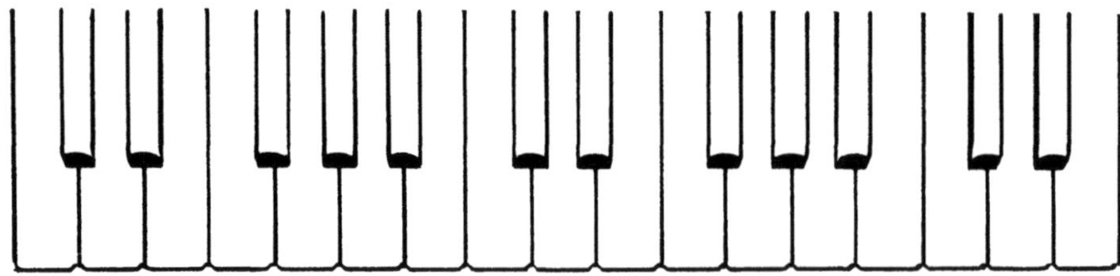

Write the Key Signature for E Major.

B Major Scale

Write the B Major Scale on the staff for the Right Hand, ascending and descending. Write the necessary sharps in front of the notes.

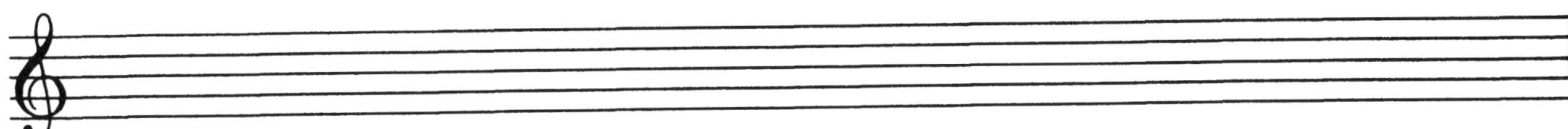

Write the fingering on the keyboard for the B Major Scale for the Right Hand.

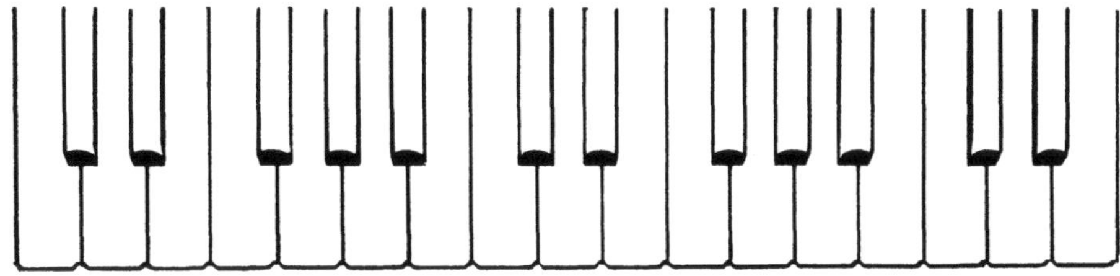

Write the B Major Scale on the staff for the Left Hand, ascending and descending.

Write the fingering on the keyboard for the B Major Scale for the Left Hand.

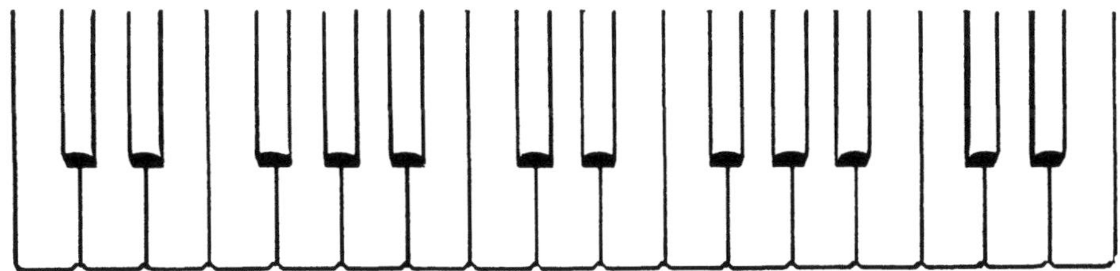

Write the Key Signature for B Major.

F.D.L.324

F Sharp Major Scale

Write the F Sharp Major Scale on the staff for the Right Hand, ascending and descending. Write the necessary sharps in front of the notes.

Write the fingering on the keyboard for the F Sharp Major Scale for the Right Hand.

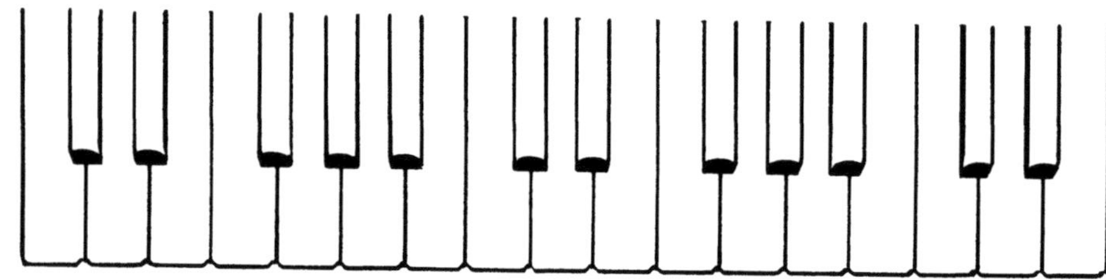

Write the F Sharp Major Scale on the staff for the Left Hand, ascending and descending.

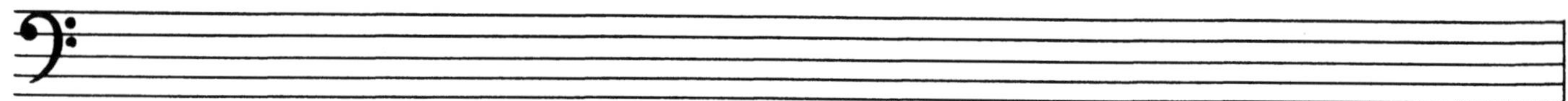

Write the fingering on the keyboard for the F Sharp Major Scale for the Left Hand.

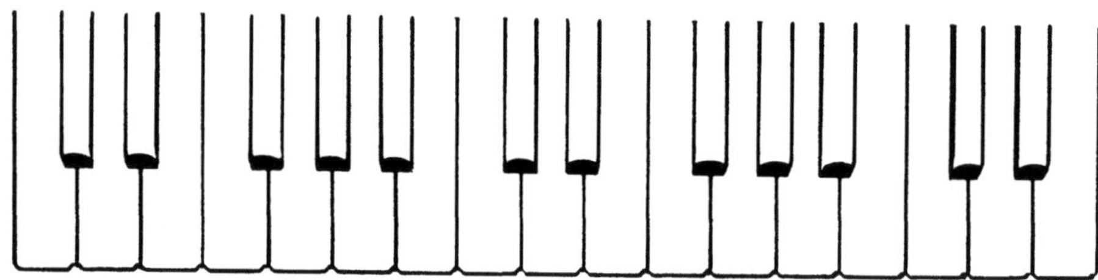

Write the Key Signature for
F♯ Major.

C Sharp Major Scale

Write the C Sharp Major Scale on the staff for the Right Hand, ascending and descending. Write the necessary sharps in front of the notes.

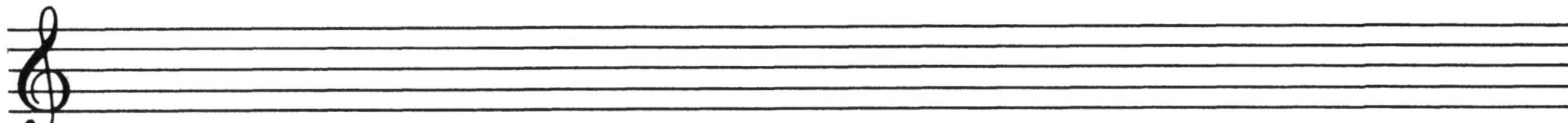

Write the fingering on the keyboard for the C Sharp Major Scale for the Right Hand.

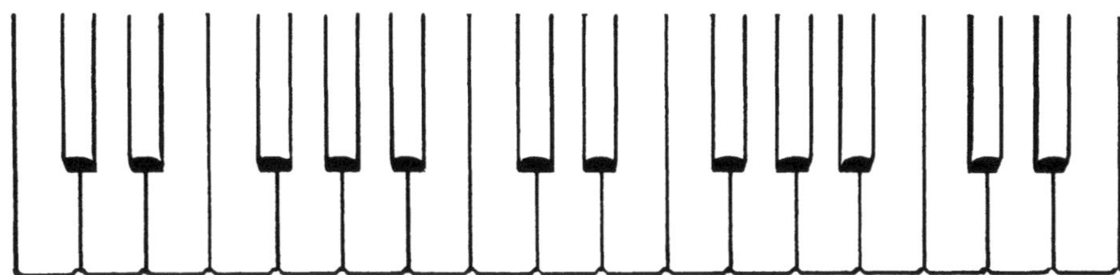

Write the C Sharp Major Scale on the staff for the Left Hand, ascending and descending.

Write the fingering on the keyboard for the C Sharp Major Scale for the Left Hand.

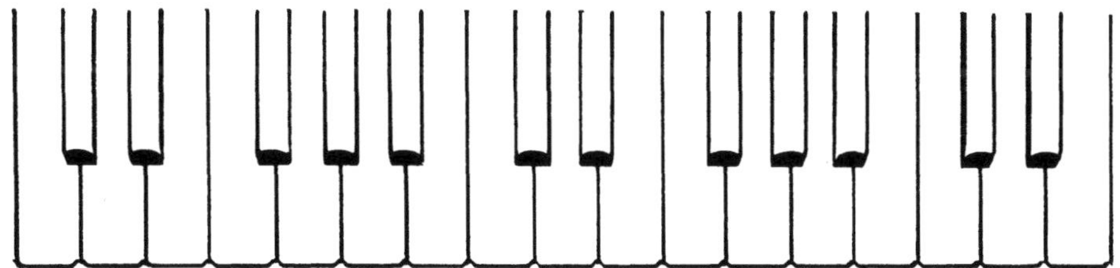

Write the Key Signature for C♯ Major.

F Major Scale

As you write the flat scales you will note that each scale starts on the fourth tone of the preceding scale and uses a new flat on the fourth tone of the new scale.

Write the F Major Scale on the staff for the Right Hand, ascending and descending. Write the necessary flats in front of the notes.

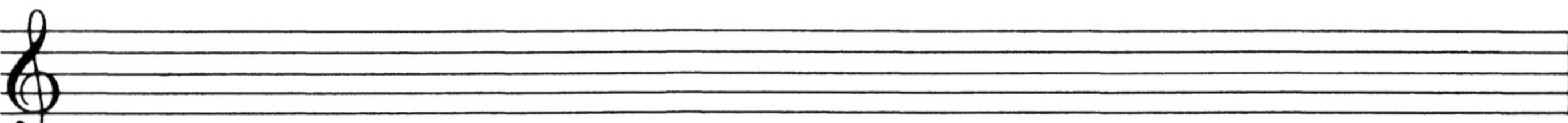

Write the fingering on the keyboard for the F Major Scale for the Right Hand.

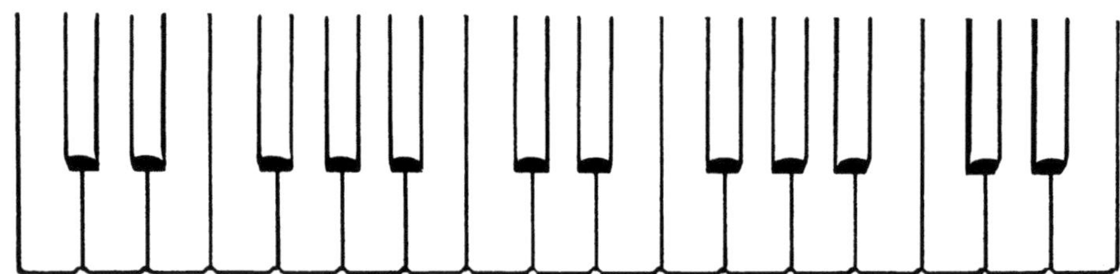

Write the F Major Scale on the staff for the left hand, ascending and descending.

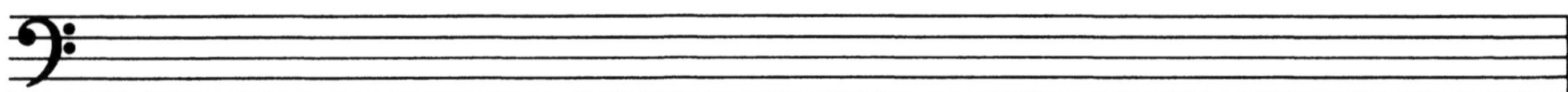

Write the fingering on the keyboard for the F Major Scale for the Left Hand.

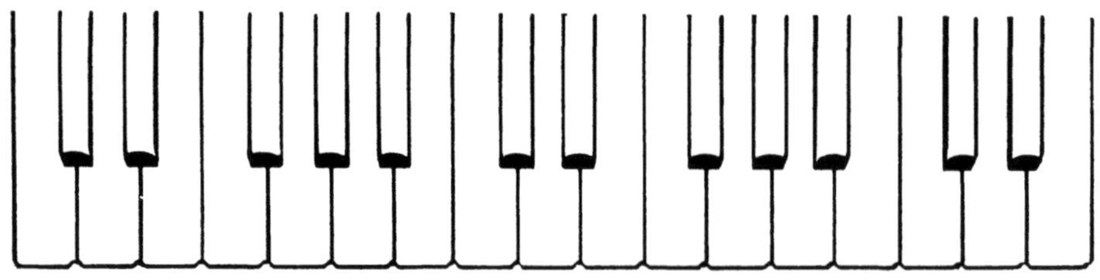

Write the Key Signature for
F Major.

B Flat Major Scale

Write the B Flat Major Scale on the staff for the Right Hand, ascending and descending. Write the necessary flats in front of the notes.

Write the fingering on the keyboard for the B Flat Major Scale for the Right Hand.

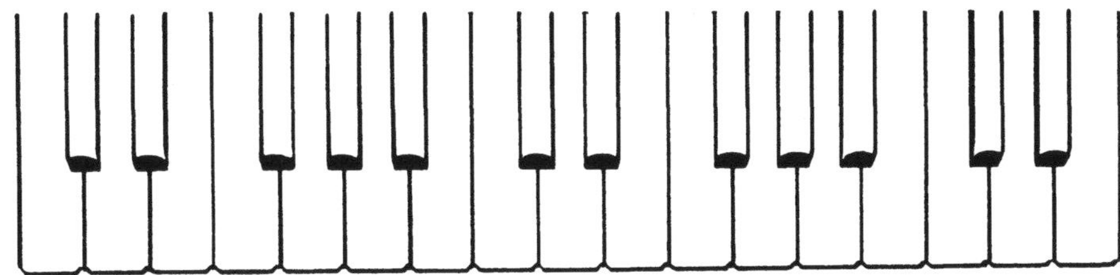

Write the B Flat Major Scale on the staff for the Left Hand.

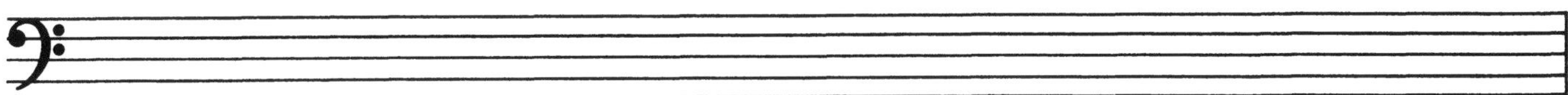

Write the fingering on the keyboard for the B Flat Major Scale for the Left Hand.

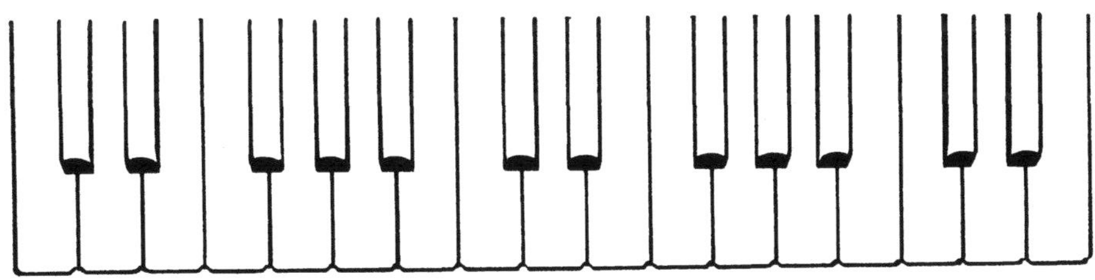

Write the Key Signature for B♭ Major.

E Flat Major Scale

Write the E Flat Major Scale on the staff for the Right Hand, ascending and descending.   Write the necessary flats in front of the notes.

Write the fingering on the keyboard for the E Flat Major Scale for the Right Hand.

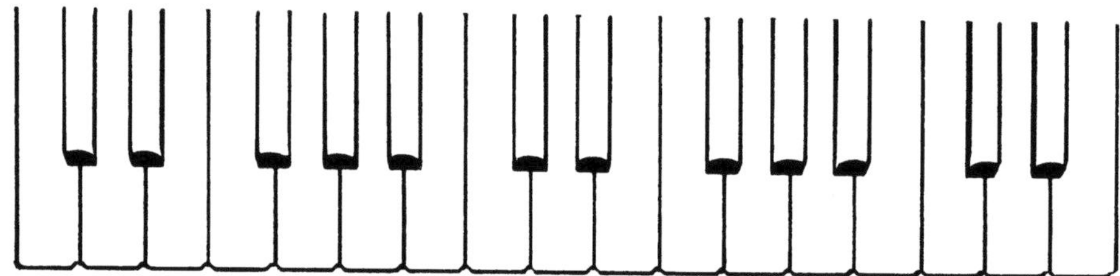

Write the E Flat Major Scale on the staff for the Left Hand, ascending and descending.

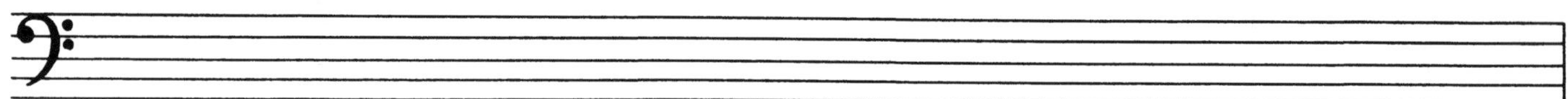

Write the fingering on the keyboard for the E Flat Major Scale for the Left Hand.

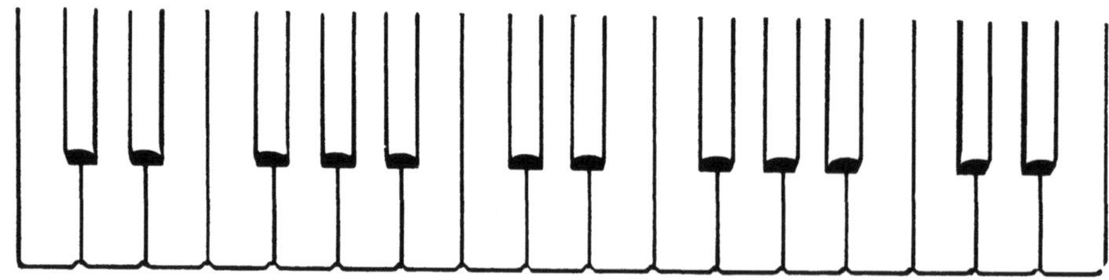

Write the Key Signature
for E♭ Major.

A Flat Major Scale

Write the A Flat Major Scale on the staff for the Right Hand, ascending and descending.   Write the necessary flats in front of the notes.

Write the fingering on the keyboard for the A Flat Major Scale for the Right Hand.

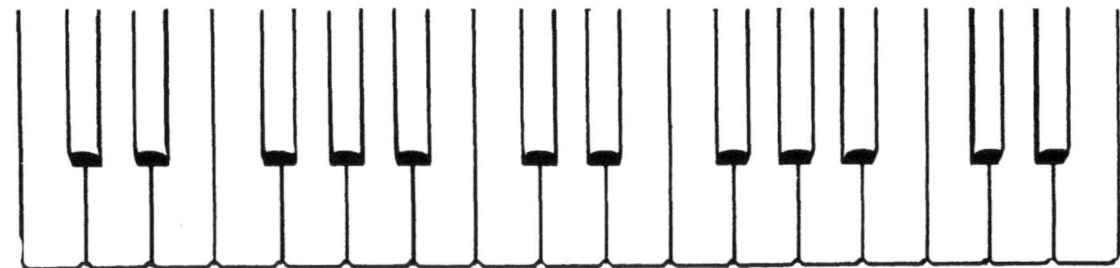

Write the A Flat Major Scale on the staff for the Left Hand, ascending and descending.

Write the fingering on the keyboard for the A Flat Major Scale for the Left Hand.

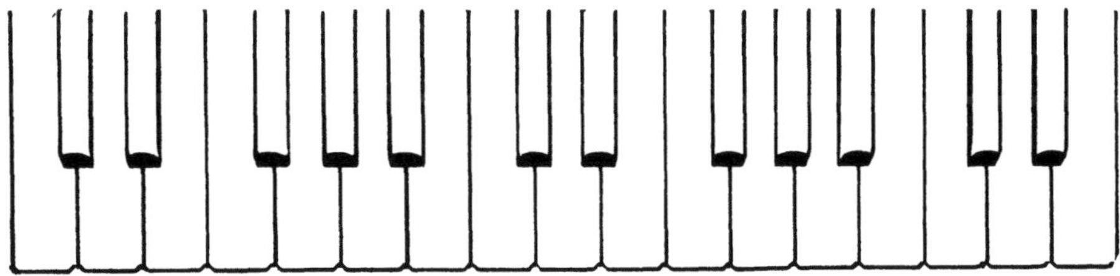

Write the Key Signature
for A♭ Major.

F.D.L.324

D Flat Major Scale

Write the D Flat Major Scale on the staff for the Right Hand, ascending and descending.   Write the necessary flats in front of the notes.

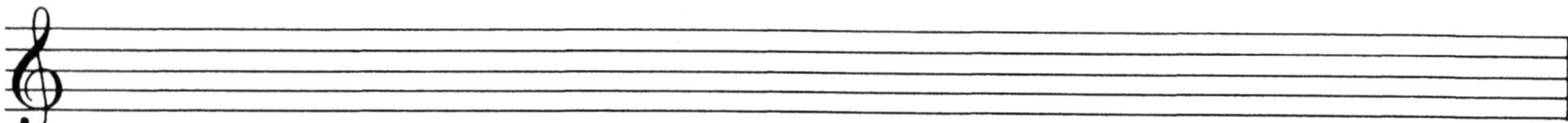

Write the fingering on the keyboard for the D Flat Major Scale for the Right Hand.

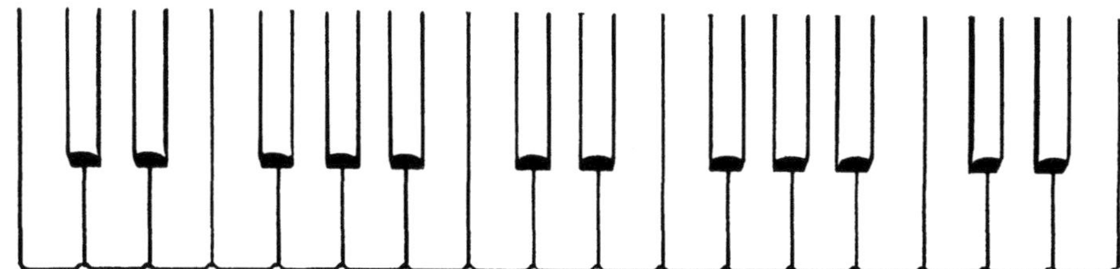

Write the D Flat Major Scale on the staff for the Left Hand, ascending and descending.

Write the fingering on the keyboard for the D Flat Major Scale for the Left Hand.

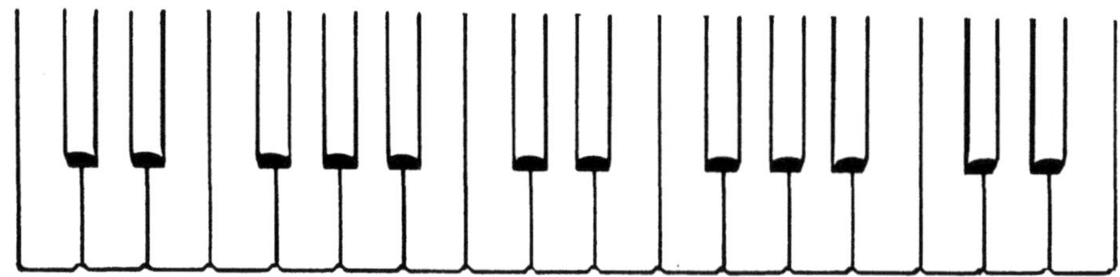

Write the Key Signature
for D♭ Major.

G Flat Major Scale

Write the G Flat Major Scale on the staff for the Right Hand, ascending and descending.   Write the necessary flats in front of the notes.

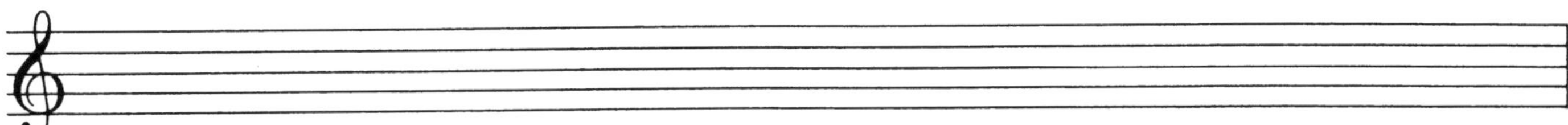

Write the fingering on the keyboard for the G Flat Major Scale for the Right Hand.

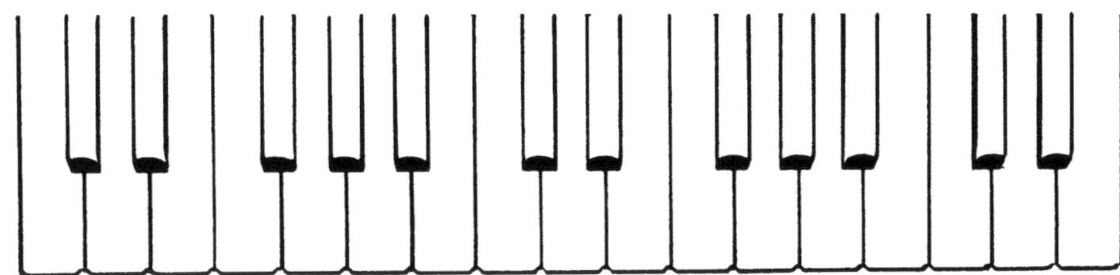

Write the G Flat Major Scale on the staff for the Left Hand, ascending and descending.

Write the fingering on the keyboard for the G Flat Major Scale for the Left Hand.

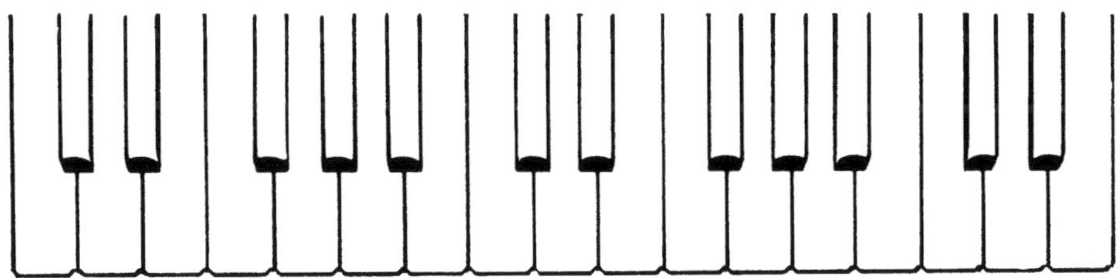

Write the Key Signature for Gb Major.

F.D.L.324

C Flat Major Scale

Write the C Flat Major Scale on the staff for the Right Hand, ascending and descending.   Write the necessary flats in front of the notes.

Write the fingering on the keyboard for the C Flat Major Scale for the Right Hand.

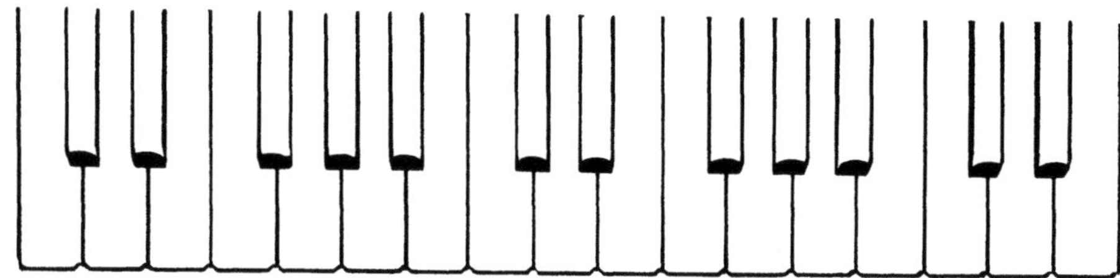

Write the C Flat Major Scale on the staff for the Left Hand, ascending and descending.

Write the fingering on the keyboard for the C Flat Major Scale for the Left Hand.

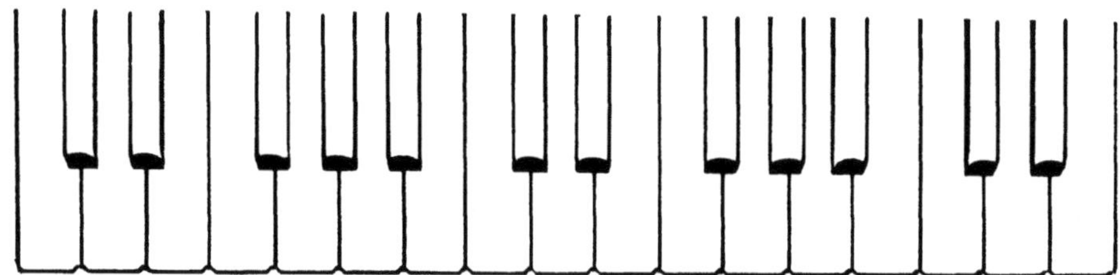

Write the Key Signature
for Cb Major.

Black Key Scales, Starting Fingers

If you can photograph the following chart in your mind, you will not have trouble remembering what finger to start black key scales on. This is NOT the scale fingering, but only the starting fingers.

Major Scales

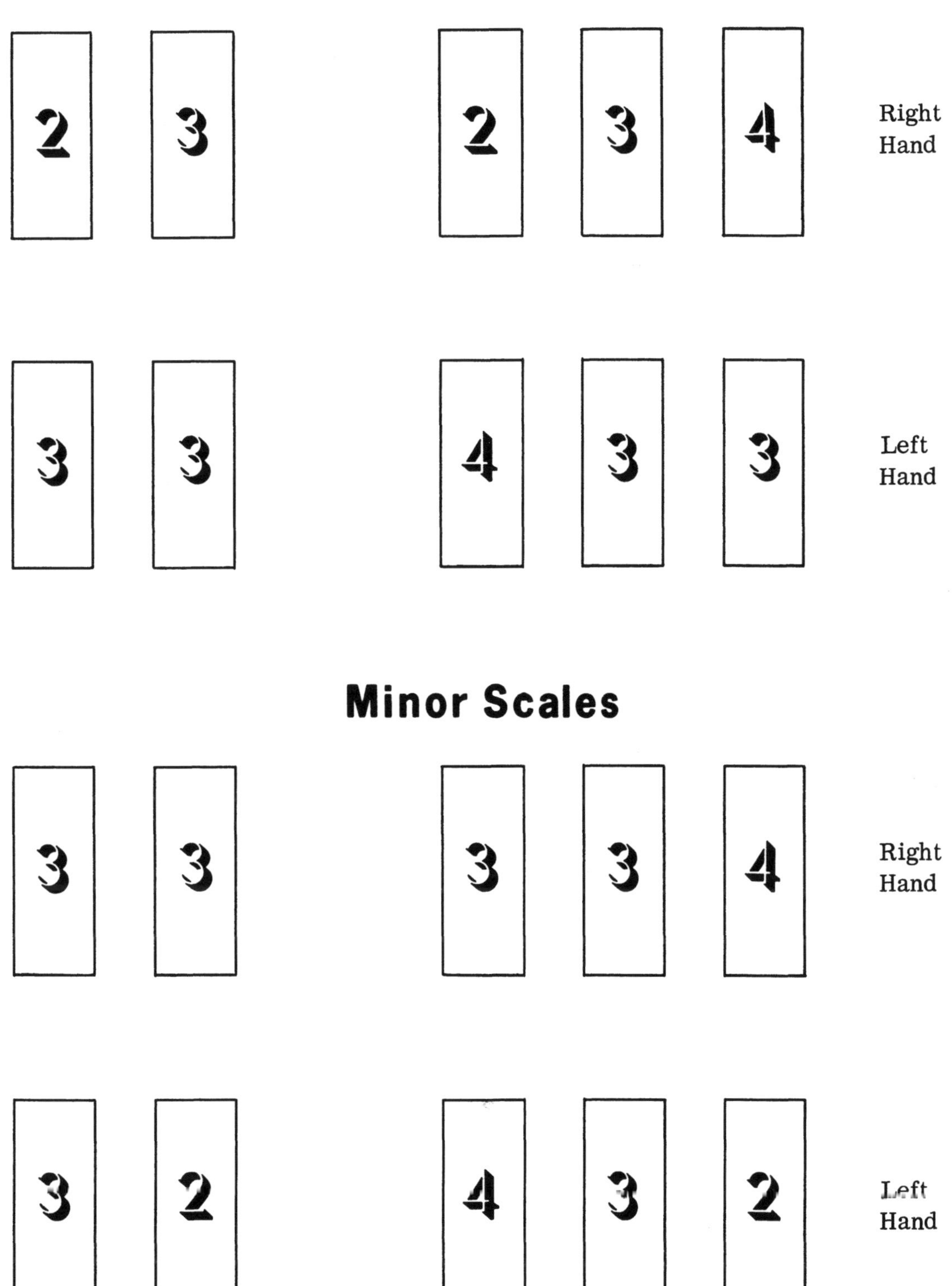

Black key scales start and end on the same finger. Note that the patterns are reversed between the hands for minor from Major.

Scale Dictionary
Major Scales

* Optional fingerings on Page 27.

F.D.L. 324

Major Scales (Cont'd)

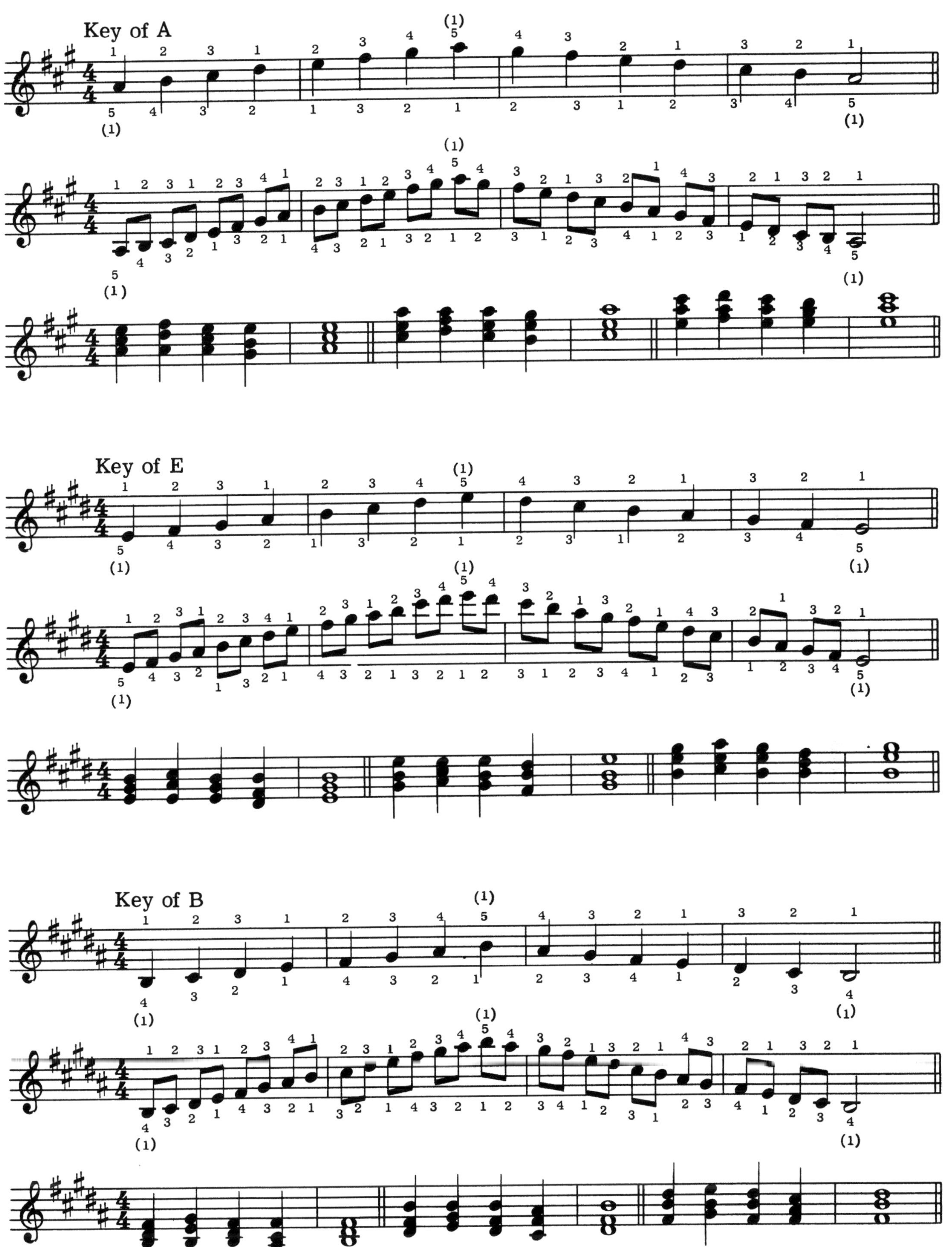

Major Scales (Cont'd)

Major Scales Cont'd)

Major Scales Cont'd)

Optional Major Scale Fingering

(Topographic)

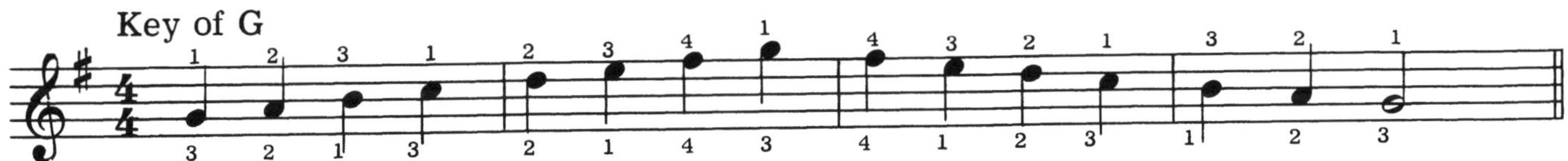

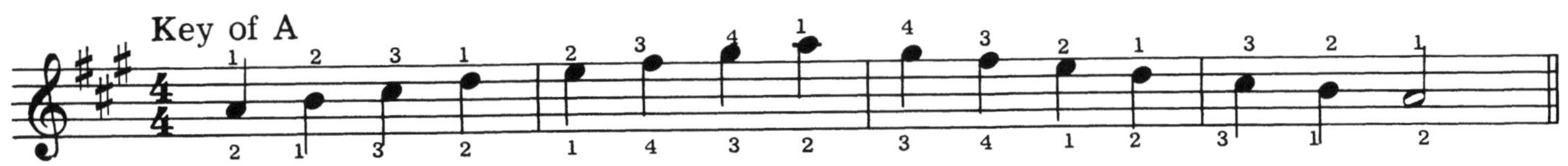

F.D.L.324

Rhythm Pattern For Developing Velocity In Scale Playing

Play in all keys.

More Scale Patterns

Play these patterns in all Major Keys.

Play up three octaves and return:

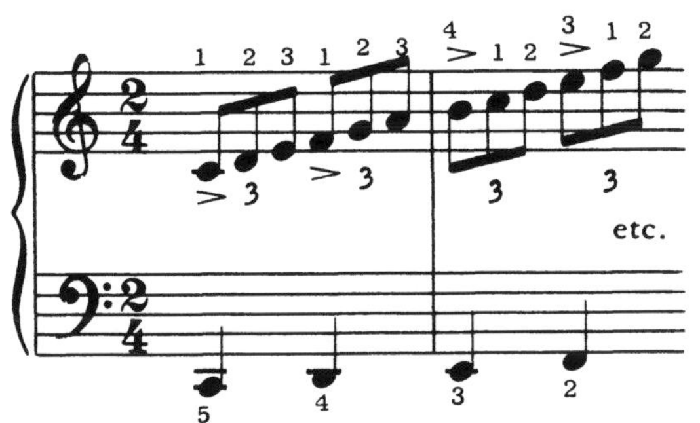

Play up three octaves and return:

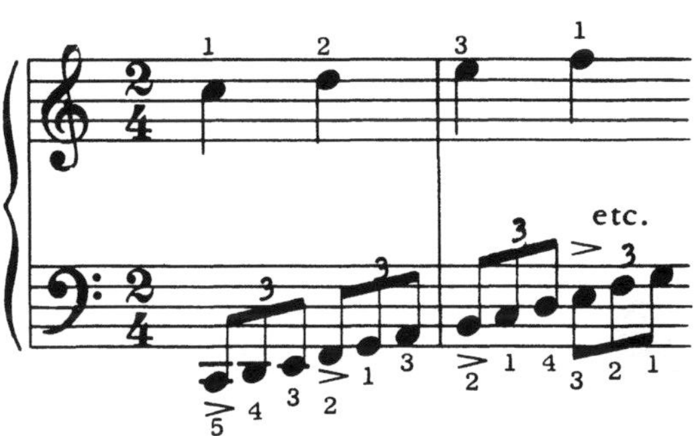

Play up four octaves and return:

Play up four octaves and return:

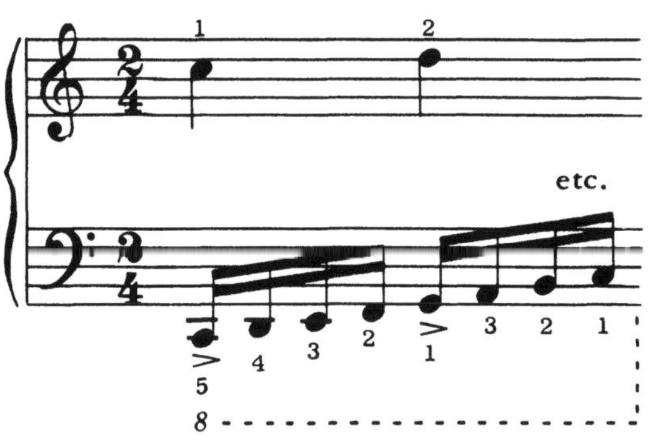

Also play these scale patterns hands together:

1. Staccato in the right hand and legato in the left.
2. Legato in the right hand and staccato in the left.

F.D.L.324

Scales and Chords Combined

Harmonizing Scales

CIRCLE OF KEYS

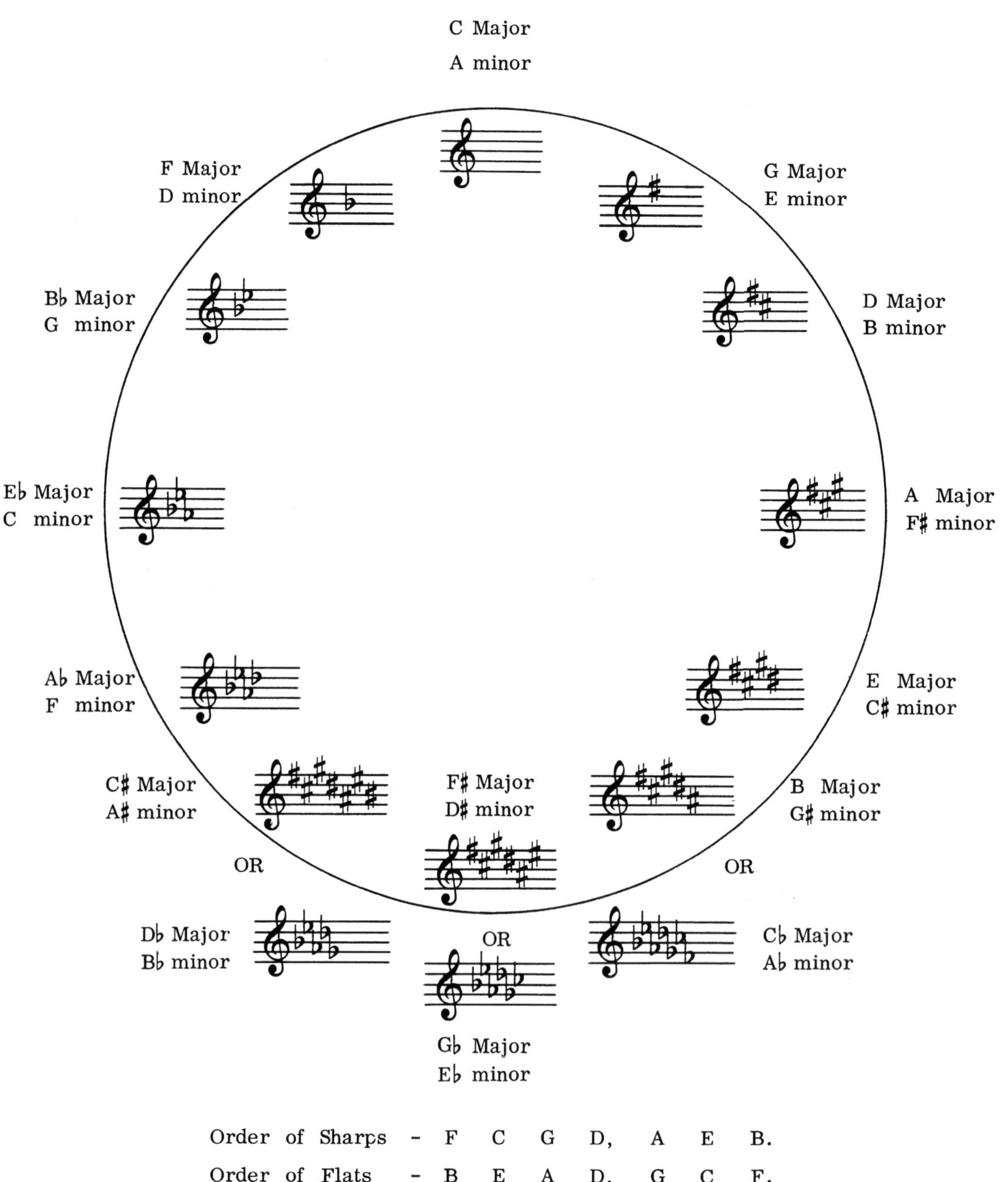

Order of Sharps - F   C   G   D,   A   E   B.

Order of Flats   - B   E   A   D,   G   C   F.